How To M Crafts from Empty Toilet Paper Rolls:

A Frugal Crafting DIY Book

Andrea Reynolds

How to Make Christmas Crafts from Empty Toilet Paper Rolls: A Frugal Crafting DIY Book Text and Photography Copyright © 2021 by Andrea Reynolds

All rights reserved. By payment of the required fees, you have been granted the non-exclusive, non-transferable right to access and read the text of this book. No part of this book may be reproduced, transmitted, downloaded, decompiled, reverse engineered, or stored in or introduced into any information storage and retrieval system, in any form or by any means, whether electronic or mechanical, not known or hereinafter invented, without the express written permission of SkyShan Publishing, LLC.

LIMITED WARRANTY: Limited warranty on this product. Skyshan Publishing warrants the product will be delivered free from defects in materials and workmanship under normal use for a period of ninety days from the date of original purchase. Skyshan Publishing will not replace the product due to any loss; this is considered out of the control of Skyshan Publishing. Great care was taken to ensure this product is accurate and presented in good faith. However, no warranty is provided, nor are results guaranteed. Having no control over the choices of materials or procedures used, neither the author nor Skyshan Publishing shall have any liability to any loss or damage caused directly or indirectly by the information contained in this book.

For information regarding permission, write to Skyshan Publishing, LLC. Att: Permissions Department, PO Box 13, Waldwick, NJ 07463

All rights reserved. Published by Skyshan Publishing, LLC

ISBN: 978-1-970106-64-0

TABLE OF CONTENTS

INTRODUCTION: 5

HOLIDAY CRACKERS TO MAKE YOURSELF 7

TOILET PAPER ROLL REINDEER 14

WAIT, I MADE A MISTAKE – I CUT OFF AN ANTLER 22

CONSTRUCTION PAPER REINDEER 26

OPTIONAL TOILET PAPER ROLL MOOSE 28

NAPKIN RING HOLDERS 33

SITTING BEAR WITH VEST 39

CONCLUSION 43

ALSO AVAILABLE FROM SKYSHAN PUBLISHING 44

ABOUT THE AUTHOR 44

Dedication: To my wonderful family who puts up with my insanity. Your support has meant the world to me.

Introduction:

No exotic crafting supplies are needed for these fantastic designs!

I have a confession to make; I love using toilet paper rolls instead of throwing them out. It's weird, but these tiny cardboard tubes are the perfect size to create unique projects. My imagination sparks with potential ideas. Pandemics notwithstanding, toilet paper rolls are in most homes.

I have two words of caution to all you potential readers before beginning. Firstly, the designs in this book are far from perfect. I am not going to sit there with tweezers and obsess over perfection. I believe in making these projects accessible to everyone. To me, perfection is found in imperfection.

Secondly, I love writing these books as I believe in making them fun. Occasionally my warped sense of humor comes out when least expected. If you want dry reading without a few humorous comments, this might not be the book for you. Hence the current subject matter.

If I haven't scared you away, welcome to this fantastic adventure in toilet paper roll crafting! This book will show you step-by-step instructions on how to create the following unique projects:

Holiday Crackers
Toilet Paper Roll Reindeer
Toilet Paper Roll Moose
Napkin Ring Holders – Multiple Ways
Sitting Bear with Vest

The Christmas season occasionally fills me with waves of anxiety, trying to make beautiful memories for my children. Even acknowledging this self-inflicted stress, finding ways to handle your mental wellbeing is vital to a happy holiday.

Crafting reminds us that the journey is important and having a tangible item at the end of the day fills you with accomplishment. Luckily these projects can be made with your youngsters to create unforgettable memories or even by yourself to destress.

Let's get crafting!

Holiday Crackers to Make Yourself

Holiday crackers have been a part of the holidays in the UK since the Victorian era around the mid-1840s. The traditional cracker contains a paper crown, a tacky joke, a snap, and a tiny little trinket. However, the sky is the limit in what you can add to your personalized cracker.

After purchasing the store-made variety for one Christmas, to say we were disappointed is an understatement. None of the snaps worked, and the quality versus the price was insane. In all honesty, with a neurotic dog who flips out during every thunderstorm, I was glad the snaps failed.

While these instructions do not include the snap, crackle, and pop of it all, these sticks are purchased at most craft stores or online retailers. Search for "Christmas Cracker Snap Strips."

These crackers come together quickly with only paper, ribbon, an empty TP roll, and glue.

Required Materials / Optional Materials (Marked as **)

For the Cracker

1-Empty Roll of Toilet Paper per Cracker

1-Piece of Copy Paper with an image printed in a Landscape orientation **or** Gift Wrap.

2- 12" (30.5 cm) ~~piece~~ Ribbon for Decoration per Cracker

Tools/Tertiary Equipment

Scissors

Glue

Color Printer / Copier to print holiday image onto paper

Computer with a program like Word to size the image

Optional Decorative Items

If you choose to utilize a custom image, you must ensure proper sizing. A picture of the family member on the cracker is a fabulous idea. However, you need to be able to see the image to have the effort appreciated.

The standard circumference of a toilet paper roll is 5.375" (13.7 cm). Please remember that I am assuming (dangerous word alert) the standard is the same in the rest of the world as the US. (If I'm wrong, please let me know in the review section while dropping a 5-star review for this literary masterpiece.) There is no need to break out π; simply wrap a piece of string around the tube, flatten the ribbon out, and measure the length.

To ensure your picture is the correct size, you can utilize your computer to make the process easier. I will be using Microsoft Word, but you can use any program based on your familiarity.

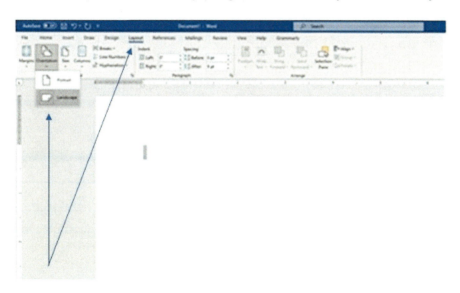

Open a blank document. Click on the "Layout" tab, click on the "Orientation" tab, and select "Landscape." Insert the picture of your choice.

Click on the "Insert" tab, then click on the "Pictures" icon, and click on "This Device" to choose the image of your choice. Be sure you know the file path of your picture's location.

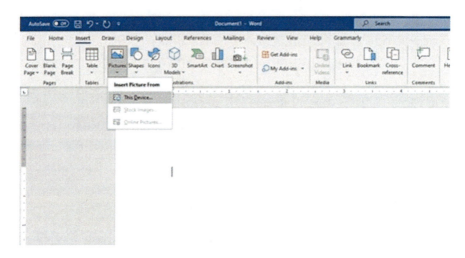

Make sure the picture is active. (Click on the picture, and the "Picture Format" tab will appear as the farthest right tab.) Click on the "Picture Format" tab. In the far right, in the "Size" section, adjust the height to 5.375 inches (13.65 cm). The width must be at least the width of the toilet paper roll. I like at least 2" (5 cm) wider than the cylinder. Print out your image—time to make the Cracker.

Trim the paper **only** to the proper height. Avoid trimming the width of the paper. (It is easier to trim excess than not have enough paper.) Place a thin layer of glue over the entirety of the outside of the toilet paper roll. Align the paper, centering the image over the cylinder, and cover the cardboard with the picture. Allow the glue to completely dry.

When the glue dries completely, grasp the roll between your thumb and forefinger at the end of the rolls on each side, and gently squeeze.

Trim the sides to be evenly spaced. Next, cut two pieces of ribbon 12" (30.5 cm) in length. Tie one string on one side in a bow. Do not be afraid to pull it tight, but go slowly to prevent ripping the paper.

Place your chosen gifts into the open side of the cracker. Some cute ideas for adults could be lottery tickets, an airplane bottle of adult libation, lipstick or nail polish for teens or adults, or individually wrapped high-end chocolates.

Tie the other end of the tube closed. Place this gift on the place setting. You can even write the recipient's name on the cracker, so there is no confusion. You don't want to accidentally give eight-year-old Bobby eighty-year-old Uncle Buck's bottle of Bourbon. If your penmanship resembles a toddler like my own, you can write the person's name on the interior of one side of the tube.

Your Christmas Cracker is ready to be demolished. The sound of tearing paper will fill your house along with the sound of laughter.

Before and after the joy.

Toilet Paper Roll Reindeer

Sometimes you just run out of crafting supplies. The kids got into the glue and spent hours making fingerprint molds, and left the top open. Never fear for this next project. The bare minimum needed for this project is two empty toilet paper rolls, scissors, and tape.

How is it possible to create a beautiful project? Personally, something about the austerity of the reindeer without embellishments appeals to me. While these instructions will include adding felt to the reindeer, the exact instructions apply to the simple design, excluding material addition.

Required Materials / Optional Materials (Marked as **)

Reindeer

2-Empty Roll(s) of Toilet Paper

**1-Piece of Felt (OR Construction Paper) Each– Dark Brown, Light Brown, Black, White, and Red

Tools/Tertiary Equipment

Scissors

**Glue, and paperclip or binder clip

Tape

Measure and cut a piece of brown felt to cover the entire roll of toilet paper. Glue the entirety of the outside of the toilet paper roll, and place the brown felt over the roll. Use paper clips or binder clips to secure the felt. Let dry.

On the second roll, cut a 1" (2.5 cm) wide piece. Push the portion of the tube to create a fold on either side. Cut the cylinder in half at one end.

Take one half of the piece of roll, and using the bottom fold pull the fold toward the top of the cardboard.

Fold the other side of the 1" (2.5 cm) roll.

Measure a piece of dark brown felt to fit the triangle at the bottom of the above picture with a ¼" (0.635 cm) additional height. Cut an extra piece of dark brown felt to fit the triangle. Next, cut 2(two) pieces of light brown felt to cover the 2(two) rectangles above the triangle.

Turn the cardboard around and glue the areas and attach the felt.

Cut out eyes, nose, and glue to the reindeer. Glue the opposite side of the brown triangle. Set aside to dry. Oh, look! My reindeer has a red nose. I wonder what I should call him.

When the reindeer's body is dry, it is time to create the body of our TP buddy. Remove the paper clips and find the top middle at the back of the tube. Measure a ½" (1.25 cm) width and cut 2 (two) ½" (1.25 cm) long incisions into the cylinder. Raise the tab slightly. Your reindeer now has a tail.

Turn the tube over to the other side. In the center of the cardboard, measure 1" (2.5 cm) wide, and cut 1" (2.5 cm) deep on either side.

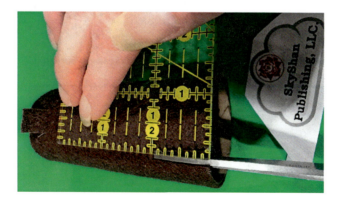

Pull the tab upward and put a bend in the tip of the front about ¼" (0.635cm). This is the neck of the reindeer.

There are some ways to make your life easier when you make your cuts when creating the legs. In the front of your reindeer, cut a 1" (2.5 cm) long strip to mirror the neck above. On the outside of these cuts, make an additional 1" (2.5 cm) long cut ¼" (0.635 cm) apart from the initial incision. (No this is not surgery) Pull these legs down, folding a ¼" (0.635 cm) tab for the feet.

Using a ruler, cut the back legs in the exact placement as the front legs. If you are using felt, cut out felt, glue, and cover the opposite side of the legs, neck, and tail. Allow to dry.

Time to turn your attention back to the head.

Sometimes bigger is not better. If you have a small pair of scissors, I recommend using them. If not, it is okay. You got this. Take your time and slowly cut out antlers. This does not have to be perfect. No two antlers are the same, and it is okay to create an organic look.

Quick Tip: Cut the antlers out slowly, working your way inward. It is okay to have a sharp edge; round it out with small snips.

Wait, I Made a Mistake – I Cut off an Antler

A moment of inattention can lead to disaster. Oopsie!

Relax! This is not the end of the world. First, turn your head over. Get some glue and cover the felt, the cardboard, and the back of the cardboard. Take a piece of tape and cover the glued area; ensure that the glue touches parts of the cardboard that does not have any glue on it. Clamp the damaged area with a binder clip or a paper clip.

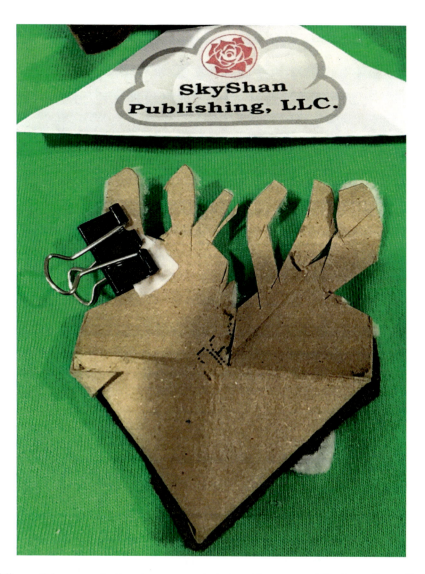

Allow this repair to dry completely. Remove binder clip after drying—time to finish assembling the reindeer.

In the front of the body, push the bottom tab into the body. Next, press each side tab into the body as well.

Repeat this step on the back of the body. Adjust the legs, so the body stands on its four legs.

When attaching the reindeer's head, two options depend upon what you have on hand.

Option one is to glue the head to the neck.

Option two is to use tape to attach the head to the neck. You will need more than these two pieces. I recommend running the adhesive covering the head to the neck.

Construction Paper Reindeer

If you don't have felt on hand, you can easily use construction paper instead. My experience with this is to make sure you use paper clips. Until the glue dries, the paper can slip.

When gluing the paper to the tube, there can be some overlap. There is no need to trim to exact measurements as the paper is thinner than felt. Make sure that you glue the overlap.

My supply of construction paper only has one shade of brown, so I used orange as the antler color. Add eyes and nose to the face.

Once dried, ensure that you cut out the tail, legs, and neck. Attach the head and enjoy your incredible creation.

Please don't disparage the antlers on the left. We can't all have a perfect rack.

Optional Toilet Paper Roll Moose

The reindeer model converts easily to a moose with only a few modifications. This is an excellent idea for moose lovers everywhere. The start of the moose head begins the same as the reindeer until this point.

Traditional depictions of moose heads show their rack of antlers as more horizontal from the head and not vertical. Therefore, the head of your animal needs an additional fold. Glue it down and hold it in place with paper clips until dry.

Cut out two pieces of dark brown felt triangles to fit the face of your moose. Cut out eyes and nose (White and black felt). Glue the face and the eyes and nose. Light brown felt should be sized and cut out.

Once the glue has dried, cut out the moose antlers, attach them to the body.

Optional Scarf Addition

Adding accessories to your reindeer and moose can add to the festive feeling of the holiday season. Santa's hats didn't look cohesive as they clashed with the antlers on each animal.

Scarves are a fantastic choice that is customizable with color choices that match your holiday decorations. If you just squinted at me, look at your decorations. The chances are that one color or type of décor is prevalent. We like what we like and tend to purchase similar themes.

I chose a primarily red scarf with a white fringe. You will need red and white felt or construction paper. Create an arch 2 3/8" (6 cm) wide and 2" (5 cm) long.

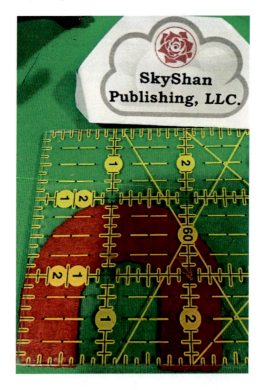

Cut out two pieces of white felt, matching the width of the ends of the scarf, and about ½" (1.25 cm) long. Cut small incisions into the white felt, about half the length, creating a fringe.

Attach the white felt to the bottom of the scarf with glue.

Slide the scarf under the head to abut the center of the arc of the scarf. Glue down the arch to the body. If you don't want to attach the scarf permanently, you can cut a notch into the back of the scarf to let it lay flat.

Napkin Ring Holders

Napkin Rings…Really? Now stay with me before you shake your head and dismiss this section out of hand. Adding a customized napkin ring holder that compliments your napkin choice can turn a humdrum place setting into a creative masterpiece.

The options to decorate these holders are endless, but I will show you three unique design choices. I hope you use this as a guide to discovering your inspiration.

A fun and shiny napkin ring can turn a plain white napkin into a festive accompaniment to your holiday meal. This napkin ring uses just yarn and a 1" (2.5 cm) wide piece of toilet paper roll.

This yarn is skinny, and you will need 4 yards (3.65 meters) of thread per napkin ring. Tie the start of the rope around the circle. Begin wrapping the yarn around the ring.

If you are wrapping the yarn, some yarn separates from the rest of the pack; use your finger to align it.

When you reach the end of the yarn, tie the end to one of the interior strings to hide the knot. Make one for each guest attending.

Utilizing fabric for the next napkin ring option is a great choice. You could even use a stained napkin from the set to make multiple rings for your friends and family to enjoy the meal you have planned.

Measure the fabric 2.5" (6.35 cm) wide. (I know the fabric appears to be 3" (7.5 cm) wide, but I did cut that down. The length should be 5 3/8" (13.5 cm).

Glue the outside of the ring. Cut notches into the side of the fabric every ¼" (0.635 cm). This process helps the fabric fold into the ring. Glue the inside of the ring, and fold the material into the ring.

Allow the glue to dry.

Felt might seem like a pedestrian choice, but it works as an excellent background for a fantastic accent piece. Glue a piece of festive colored felt to a napkin ring. Ensure you cut notches into your felt for ease of folding into the napkin ring.

I found a great bow with a bell that I tied to the inside of the ring. A boring piece turns into a formal statement.

Sitting Bear with Vest

If you're scratching your head about why this little animal needs only one TP roll and not two like the other, the answer is the orientation. This great little bear, made with only one toilet paper roll, sits vertically. The bear sitting up can support the head, but a reindeer with a rack of antlers will tip over every time.

Cover and glue a piece of felt or construction paper to a tube of TP. Let dry completely—Mark 1" (2.5 cm) around the circumference. Use scissors to cut it out.

Fold the 1" (2.5 cm) piece to create the face. Glue down if necessary and use a binder clip to hold down the center seam.

Cut out the body. The arms and legs should be ½" (1.25 cm) long and ¼" (0.635 cm) wide. Ensure the tail is cut as well to help it stand.

Cut out the bear's face—round out the bottom of the face and the ears. Add eyes, nose, and ears, and glue.

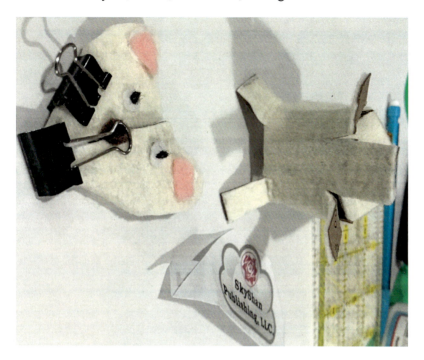

Glue the head onto the neck.

Adding embellishments to this project is a great idea. There is a lot of negative space on the body, so a tie and vest added a festive touch.

Conclusion

We've made it to the end of another crafting journey. I can't thank you enough for reading this book.

Sometimes you must be who you were born to be. I love turning something that usually gets tossed in the trash into something that will occupy you and your kids for hours. If you can look at something from a different perspective, I encourage you to embrace your creativity.

I have many other craft books planned in the coming months and years. What the next book in this series will be is anyone's guess. I can't promise when the next book will be out, as things do not always work out as planned. I hope that you will join me on other journeys.

My only request is to let others know that this book is for them by leaving a review. Unfortunately, the crafting genre is filled with "books" from people that copy and paste blogs instead of putting in the effort themselves. By using your reviewing abilities, small independent authors like myself have a chance of getting noticed.

Happy Crafting!

Also Available from SkyShan Publishing

About the Author

Andrea Reynolds has always had an incredible imagination. She is the internationally bestselling author of over thirty books. Her love of crafting has brought her more joy and peace than any other activity. She just wishes she could draw a stick figure. She is the mother of two beautiful children and one rescue dog. When not writing, her head will be found stuck in her crafting closet.

Made in United States
North Haven, CT
22 November 2024